PRAYERS FOR A FRAGILE WORLD

Prayers

· *for a* ·

Fragile

World

Written
and compiled
by

Carol Watson

Illustrations

by

Rhian Nest James

A LION BOOK

For my father

Copyright © 1991 Lion Publishing
This compilation and prayers by the author copyright © 1991 Carol Watson
Illustrations copyright © 1991 Rhian Nest James

Published by
Lion Publishing plc
Sandy Lane West, Oxford, England
ISBN 0 7459 1949 9
Albatross Books Pty Ltd
PO Box 320, Sutherland, NSW 2232, Australia
ISBN 0 7324 0503 3

First edition 1991
10 9 8 7 6 5 4 3 2

Acknowledgments
With special thanks to John and Sandra Bazlinton, His Honour Judge
Christopher Compston, Nabil Shehadi, Prudence Lynch, Anne Wright,
Rosie Anstice and the Reverend Richard Adfield.

Scripture taken from the HOLY BIBLE; NEW INTERNATIONAL
VERSION. Copyright © 1973, 1978, 1984 by International Bible Society. Used
by permission of Hodder and Stoughton Limited.

A catalogue record for this book is available
from the British Library

Printed and bound in Slovenia

Contents

Foreword

The Bible tells us that in the beginning God created a
beautiful world for people to enjoy. He gave us trees and
flowers, mountains and valleys, rivers and streams, and
wonderful animals to keep us company. He created the sun
to give us warmth and light, and the rain to help our crops
to grow. Everything God created was in perfect balance, so
that we, his children, could have everything we need.
Sometimes we forget to thank God for all the good things
he gave us.

For many years we have been destroying much of what
God gave us by our greed and selfishness. All over the
world people suffer because of war, poverty, sickness and
famine. We pollute and abuse our environment and the
animals given to our care. We wonder why things have
gone wrong. But do we ever stop to ask God to forgive us?

Why have we messed up the world? In our desire for
friends, success and money, many of us have forgotten
about loving, caring and giving to others. But God loves us,
and he sent his Son Jesus to show us how to care. God
wants to help us. Whoever and wherever we are, God
would like to hear our prayers.

If we want things in this world to get better, it is we
who have to change and we need to ask God's help to
change us. We need to learn to love him *and* others just as
he loves and cares for us. God knows what is best for us; if
we try to live in a way that will please him we will have a
future full of hope.

Carol Watson

THANK YOU, LORD...

In the beginning God created the heavens and the earth...
And God saw all that he had made, and it was very good.

Genesis 1:1,31

God's world is good.
We like it.
He made the sun to give us light
and to keep us warm.
The trees give us fruit.
God's world is full of twinkly stars,
beautiful flowers and furry animals.
God made us.
He made this world.
God wants us to be happy.
God loves us.

Yvette Leavy (age 5)

Thank you, Lord God,
for the stunning colours of nature.

Thank you...
   for the rich brown of the earth
   and the soothing greens
   of grass and leaves.

Thank you...
   for the vibrant, golden yellows
   of flower petals
   and the gentle pink of frothy blossom.

Thank you...
   for the clear, cool blue of the sky
   and the warm glow of a red sunset.

Thank you...
   for the inky blackness of the night sky
   and the sparkling white light
   of the twinkling stars.

Thank you, Lord, for your glorious creation.

When I consider your heavens,
the work of your fingers,
the moon and the stars,
which you have set in place,
what is man that you are mindful of him,
mankind that you care for him?
You made him a little lower than the heavenly beings
and crowned him with glory and honour.
You made him ruler over the works of your hands;
you put everything under his feet:
all flocks and herds,
and the beasts of the field, the birds of the air,
and the fish of the sea,
all that swim the paths of the seas.
O Lord, Our Lord,
how majestic is your name in all the earth!

Psalm 8:3-9

Great God, I'm glad you made the earth the way you did.
The moon is empty with only rocks and dust,
but we have rivers, trees, and prairies,
deserts, canyons, flowers, and green grass.
The astronauts in their capsules say
the earth is full of colour, the moon is not.
And so, O God,
for the beautiful planet Earth
you made for us,
I praise you.

Thank you, Lord,
for our world—
for the sun and moon.
Thank you, Lord,
for the seas and trees.
Thank you for the animals,
like birds and bees.
Mostly, Lord, thank you for us,
that we are alive and that we
have such a beautiful world.
Amen

Naomi Smith

Praisèd be my Lord God for all his creatures,
and especially our brother the sun,
who brings us the day and brings us the light;
fair is he and shines with a great splendour;
O Lord, he signifies to us thee.

Praisèd be my Lord for our sister the moon,
and for the stars, which he has set clear
and lovely in the heaven.

Praisèd be my Lord for our brother the wind,
and for air and cloud, calms and all weather,
by which thou upholdest life in all creatures.

Praisèd be my Lord for our sister water,
who is very serviceable unto us
and humble and precious and clean.

Praisèd be my Lord for our brother fire,
through whom thou givest light in the darkness;
and he is bright and pleasant and very mighty and strong.

Praisèd be my Lord for our mother the earth,
who doth sustain and keep us,
and bringest forth divers fruits
and flowers of many colours, and grass.

Praise ye and bless ye the Lord,
and give thanks unto him,
and serve him with great humility.
Amen

Francis of Assisi (1182–1226)

Dear Lord, thank you for the sun.
Thank you for its light, its heat, its power.
Thank you for the radiant light of spring sunshine
which brings the world back to life after
a long, cold winter.
Thank you for the healing warmth of the sun
that makes us feel better when we have been ill.
Thank you for pretty dappled sunlight
flickering through the trees of a leafy wood.
Thank you that, just as the sun lights up the world
and spreads its warmth through the earth, so your
love heals us and lights up our lives.

Dear Father in heaven, you made the sun
and it's been lighting up this earth I live on
for millions of years.
If the sun went out, we would be in darkness
and coldness always.
Your son, Jesus, said "I am the Light of the World."
We need him just as we need the sun in the sky.
I would like everyone to believe that Jesus
is the Light of the World.

Father,
Thank you for the sun
which helps things grow.
Please help us always
to grow in love with you.
Amen

Alexander Carter (age 9)

Lord God,
Thank you for the sun.
Thank you for its warmth and light.

Thank you that when the
sun shines, everybody seems to
be much happier.

Help me to shine like the sun,
and bring warmth, light and
happiness into people's lives.

Dear God,
It's fun
in the sun.
Thank you.

C.C.

Father God,
We thank you for the rain
which helps our crops to grow.

We thank you for raging storms
which remind us of your mighty power.

We thank you for the cool,
refreshing raindrops
which fall after a time of hot sun.

We thank you for the fresh scent of
flowers and trees after a shower of rain.

We thank you, Lord, for giving us
water for our daily needs.

Sing to the Lord, exalt him high,
who spreads his clouds along the sky;
there he prepares the fruitful rain,
nor lets the drops descend in vain.

Isaac Watts (1674–1748)

Yesterday the sky grew black
and the wind and rain
rattled the windows.
I was frightened, God.
But then I knew
that you're the only one
with the power
to create storms,
that this is your way
of sending water
to make crops grow
and give us food.
Thank you, God,
for caring for us.

Lord God, thank you for the gentle
raindrops which clean and water
our world.

Our Father in heaven,
we praise you for the gift of rain;
thank you for giving rain
to make the trees and flowers grow;
thank you for sending rain
so that we may have water to drink;
thank you for the summer rain
that cools the hot, dry earth.

Lord God, we praise and thank you for the spring.
We thank you for the young buds thrusting up out of the earth,
for the fresh blossom nodding on the trees
and the new petals unfolding gently in the sunshine.

We praise and thank you that every year
what seemed to be dead comes to life once more.
Help us to remember that you give the promise
of new life and hope to those who believe in you.
In Jesus' name,
Amen

Father,
Thank you for summer.
Thank you for shiny leaves.
Thank you for beautiful flowers.
Thank you for the warm sunshine.
Thank you for the birds that sing.
Amen

Anjali Assumall (age 8)

We praise you, Lord, for the beauty of autumn...
for the rich, red and golden leaves,
which fall gently from the trees
and crunch beneath our feet.
We thank you for this time when the sleepy earth
winds down for its winter rest.
It reminds us that we, too, should slow down sometimes,
rest a while, and prepare ourselves for a new season of hope.

Thank you, Lord,
for the white, gentle snow that
thickly covers the ground.

Thank you for the falling raindrops that
pitter patter on umbrellas.

Thank you for the robin that cheers
people with its happy song.

Thank you, Lord, for winter.
Amen

Debbie Simmonds (age 11)

Dear Lord,
Thank you for the spring,
the dew wet on the grass,
the flowers peeping up through the moist ground,
revealing their beautiful and bright colours.

Thank you, Lord, for the long summer days,
for the drifting wisps of white cloud high up in the sky,
and the bright, summer sun.

We thank you, Lord, for the autumn leaves
in piles on the ground,
the juicy fruit in plenty scattered all around.

We thank you for the winter,
the crisp, white snow,
the season of reflection
before the new year starts.

Kate Leckie (age 11)

Thank you, Lord, for trees.
Thank you for mighty forests of tall firs
and gentle, green woods with leafy branches
that sigh in the wind.
Thank you for boughs heavy with sweet-scented blossom
and fresh, green leaves waving in the breeze.
Thank you for the cool shade of trees on a hot summer's day
and the homes they give to the creatures all around.

We praise you, Lord, for the miracle of trees...
how their roots reach deep down into the earth,
keeping them strong and firm as they stretch upwards
to the light.
Help us to be like the tall trees,
keep us rooted in your love,
so we can stand strong and steady
in the storms of life.

We thank you, God, for the trees
which give us oxygen,
and the flowers which make
the world look pretty.
Amen

Anne Davis (age 9)

Dear Father in heaven,
Thank you for your wonderful countryside,
where all the wild animals live,
and for the trees which sway from side to side
in the wind, spreading their seeds far and wide.
Amen

Claire Fudge (age 10)

When I look at
the frail petals of a flower,
the intricate veins on a leaf
and the tiny buds gently opening,
I wonder at the miraculous details of nature.

I praise and thank you, Lord, that you
love us so much that you created
all this beauty for our enjoyment.

Help us to love and care for the
things you gave us, just as you
love and care for us.

We praise you, Lord, for the miracle
of life and growth.

Every plant needs just the right amount
of sun, rain and air
so that it can be strong and healthy.
If there is not the right balance,
the plant becomes weak and cannot bear fruit.

We praise you that you created the world
with just the right atmosphere
for people to live and grow.

Father, help us to preserve this perfection in nature,
and to keep the right balance in our own lives,
so we can grow strong and healthy too.
Amen

Lord God, we thank you for all the animals that share our world.
Thank you for the different kinds you have made:
    wild animals in the jungles,
    farm animals in the countryside,
    gentle animals we keep as pets.
Help us to care for them and protect them
from those who treat them cruelly.

God our Father,
We thank you for all the beautiful creatures
you have given us in this world...
the sleek and gentle grey seal,
the cunning fox
and the swift-footed leopard.

Help us not to take them for granted
and destroy your creation.
Amen

Nadia Farid (age 11)

All things bright and beautiful,
All creatures great and small,
All things wise and wonderful
The Lord God made them all.

He gave us eyes to see them,
And lips that we might tell,
How great is God Almighty,
Who has made all things well.

Cecil Frances Alexander (1818–95)

Dear Lord,
Thank you for animals.
Sometimes when we are lonely, animals can comfort us.
Animals are wonderful and need lots of love and care.
Help people who treat animals badly
to see what they are doing to your creatures.

Christopher Thomaidis (age 11)

Dear Lord,
Thank you for birds.
Thank you for giving them
voices to sing and chirp
their lovely songs.

Christopher Thomaidis (age 11)

Father,
When I wake up in the morning
and see my cat beside me,
I thank you for creating her.
Amen

Nicola McGrath (age 11)

Father,
Thank you for life.
Thank you for people.
Thank you for all the races of the world.
You made us different shapes, sizes and colours—
each with a language and culture of our own.
Although we are so different,
yet we are the same.
We are all human beings.
We share the same needs, desires, hopes and hurts.

Thank you, Lord, that
whatever our race or colour,
we are all your creation
and you love us.

Help us to love each other.
In Jesus' name,
Amen

Dear Lord, we thank you for...
   brains to think, reason and learn,
   eyes to see the loveliness of nature,
   ears to hear the birds sing,
   arms to hold and comfort each other,
   legs to run and jump for joy
   and mouths to shout and sing your praise.
Thank you, Lord, for the miracle of the human body.
Help us never to take it for granted.

Father God,
Thank you for our bodies.
Help us to keep them fit, healthy and active
so that we can work for you.
May we keep our minds clean
and our hearts warm and open,
so that we can share your love with those around us.

God our Creator,
for our bodies which live and breathe and grow,
for our hands which make and create,
for our feet which run and jump and play,
we give you thanks.

Thank you, Lord, for all the countries of the world.
Thank you for all the contrasts
in nature that they offer...

...the steamy, tropical jungles
and the dry, searing heat of the desert.

...the tall, rugged mountains
and the lush, green valleys below.

Thank you for the differences
between each country,
and the many things
we can learn and discover about each other.

Lord, we give thanks for all the different animals,
crops, minerals and resources that we find in
all the countries of the world.
We thank you that no matter how rich or poor,
all countries have something to offer
and to learn from one another.
We thank you that you provide for the world's needs,
if only we could all learn to share.
Amen

FATHER, FORGIVE US...

'Father, forgive them,
for they know not what they do.'

Luke 23:34

Lord,
Forgive me when I want things
that I do not need,
just because everyone else has them.

Help me to remember that there are
others all over the world
who have nothing—and that if we
were all more loving and less selfish
they would have what they need.

My friend has a new bike.
Now I want one like hers.

I know I don't need one;
my old one still works.
I'm just being greedy.

Lord, forgive me.
Help me to think of others
who have less than me,
not those who have more.

Heavenly Father,
Forgive us for what we have done to your world.
You gave us beauty, peace,
harmony and love.
We have replaced these with greed,
violence, hatred and war.
We selfishly destroy your creation,
and care little for each other's needs.

We are sorry, Lord,
for now we see the results of our sin.
Help us to realize that we must do everything
we can to right the wrong,
and to work together to save what you created.

I want a CD player,
   you want a video,
      we both want a computer.

She needs food,
   he needs shelter,
      they both need...help.

Forgive us, Lord, for our blindness
to the needs of others.
Forgive us, Lord, for our greed.

Soften our hearts and make us more aware
of the pain and suffering all around us.
Teach us to give, rather than to take.
In Jesus' name,
Amen

Lord,
We've messed it up...your world.
We are destroying your creation
with our selfish demands
and our thoughtless actions.
Forgive us, Lord.
Help us to discover
what is really important in life.
Help us to see sense,
before it is too late.

Lord,
I said I'd go shopping for the
old lady round the corner.
Then my friend came round.
We watched a video instead.
Now, I feel terrible.

Father, forgive me for being selfish.
Help me to put others before myself
even when I find it really hard.

Father, we know that you want to give us
your peace and joy in our lives.
But what is happening to people nowadays?
All we think about is getting on,
having money and buying things.
We believe this
will make us happy,
but then we are still not content.

Lord, forgive us for getting it all wrong.
Help us to see what really matters
is love, friendship and caring for others.

Help us to realize that no amount of money
will bring us the security
that your love brings.

We are sorry that so often
we let you down.

Dear God, I'm sorry.
I spent all my pocket money on sweets.
I know I should have given some
to the poor children
who have nothing to eat.
Forgive me.

We want...
    money,
    fame,
    power.

We lie,
    cheat,
    and hurt people
    to get what we want.

Forgive us, Lord.
Help us to change.
Make us more worthy of your love.

Dear God,
Please forgive us for ruining your creation.
Forgive us for the many things we do
that are dishonest and unjust.
Forgive us for killing your only son
when he came to earth.
Please help us to worship you
and help us to restore your earth to its former glory.
Amen

Neil Third and William Hare (age 13)

A rap for forgiveness

Forgive those who do things wrong,
perhaps with these words they will go along.

If you take good notice of this rhyme,
you might stop committing a crime.

Chill out.

If you know what's good for you,
you'd better stop murdering, or stealing too.

A seat should be shared by black and white,
without them having a great, big fight.

You should do these things without being told,
before love and care does grow too old.

Try to stay to God's commands,
and not be ruled by your own demands.

Oh yeah!

Daniel Constantinou (age 13)

Father,
How can you bear it?
What must you think
when you see...
    the anger
    the hatred,
    the killing
    and the endless wars?

What must you feel
when you see...
    the bombs,
    the guns,
    the tanks
    and the missiles?

Can you forgive us for
the cruelty we inflict on one another?

We are sorry, Lord.
We are not worthy of your love.

Forgive us, Lord,
for money and greed,
and pointless wars
against other creeds.

In some countries
black and white fight,
green is becoming brown
as our environment breaks down.

Help us, Lord.

James Mclachlan (age 13)

Father,
forgive
the tension,
frustration,
anger,
jealousy
and spite...
that is in our lives.

Help us to love our enemies,
forgive those that harm us,
and try to understand
each other's problems.

Lord, sometimes I wonder
what the earth was like
when it was all new.
I wonder—and then I'm sad,
because I see your beautiful rivers
all brown and scummy,
and the lakes, slimy green
with old tyres sticking out.
And I see junky cars piled in fields.
Sometimes I forget
and throw down empty pop cans
and sweet wrappers, without thinking.
Lord, I'm sorry for the times
I spoil your world.
Show me what I can do
to make it beautiful again.

Dear Lord,
You freely gave us a beautiful world.
Please forgive us for making it ugly.
Help us to restore and preserve its beauty.

Christopher Compston

Father, forgive us our carelessness
and the way we abuse the
good things you give us.
Help us to turn away from
our selfish desires
towards the needs of others.

God,
Father of all,
Creator of clean waters,
blue skies, of sparkling snow
and yellow wheatfields.
Forgive us for the waste we dump,
the forests we destroy,
the greyness we create.

Emoshioke Imoedemhe (age 11)

Lord God,
We are finding out
that this planet and its elements
are held in a balance
which is more complex
than we ever thought possible.
Forgive us, Lord, for our pride
in thinking that we could control
this world that you created,
without consulting you.
In Jesus' name,
Amen

John Bazlinton

Dear loving Father,
We are sorry...
for destroying your world.

We are sorry...
for the pollution of the sea
and for pouring gallons of oil into it every year.

We are sorry...
for the car fumes in the atmosphere,
for acid rain and all the things it destroys.

We are sorry...
for the destruction of animals and their homes,
and for litter in the streets.

Please help us to make our world a better place.
Amen

Geraldine Murphy (age 10)

Forgive us, Lord,
for the pollution we make,
even when we know
the world is at stake.
Amen

Timothy Goldsmith (age 13)

One man drops a piece of litter,
One ship dumps ten loads of waste.
Which is worse, Lord?

Sorry we have messed up your world, Lord.
Please forgive our stupidity.
Amen

Trevor Smith (age 13)

Dear Lord,
Please help to save the ozone layer,
because it is dying forever and ever.
If we can't save our big, wide planet,
you give it a try, we know you can do it.
We need your help, so come on friend,
let's work together before it's the end.

Anonymous child

The sun shines down on the park.
Birds sing, and pretty, sweet-smelling flowers
nod gently in the breeze.
As I walk along I thank you, Lord,
for the beauty of your creation.

Later, I return.
Blaring radios drown the birdsong,
foul-smelling litter is strewn across the flowers,
and the air is filled with traffic fumes.

How quickly we spoil the loveliness of nature.
Forgive us, Lord, for our carelessness.
Help us to appreciate what you have given us
and to look after it well.

Lord,
You made the world,
but look how we are tearing it apart!
Forgive us, Lord.
We cut down trees
and destroy animals' homes.
Amen

Hayley Bentley (age 10)

Please God,
Forgive all those who are cruel to animals—
and those who harm them for their own pleasure.
You created the birds and animals for our enjoyment.
You gave them life, as you gave us life.
Help us to care for them just as you care for us.

Dear Lord,
We are deeply sorry for the animals
we have killed, either for fun
or for their fur, that are now
endangered species.
We pray that those that remain will breed
and no longer be in danger of dying out.
Forgive us for doing this to your creation.

Katy Mather (age 10)

. . . *f o r   h a r m i n g   o u r   b o d i e s*

Forgive us, Lord, when we do things which harm our bodies,
like smoking, getting drunk, eating too much or taking drugs.
Help us to remember that you created us
to be fit, healthy·and strong.

We are sorry for our weaknesses and bad habits.
Help us to be more self-disciplined
and to stop hurting ourselves.
In Jesus' name,
Amen

Lord,
I'm worried.
I have a friend
who is into drugs.
He thinks it's clever
and he wants me to join in.
He teases me and says I'm scared.

Forgive me, Lord.
I was tempted to try.
It's not easy
being the only one to say no.

Help me to be strong
when the others laugh.
Help them to realize
that they are harming themselves.
Forgive them, too, Lord.

LORD, TEACH US TO CARE...

'A new command I give you: Love one another.
As I have loved you, so you must love one another.'

John 13:34,35

Hello God,
Can you hear me
above all the noise?
It's us fighting one another.
Please help us to stop all our wars.
Amen

Josephine Davies (age 9)

Dear heavenly Father,
Wars have been raging between
countries for years, and many lives
have been lost for no reason at all.

People are vain and greedy
and want more
power and money.

Please help us to be happy
with what we've got.
Amen

Katie Goodwin (age 10)

Lord, make me an instrument of thy peace;
Where there is hatred, let me sow love;
Where there is injury, pardon;
Where there is discord, union;
Where there is doubt, faith;
Where there is despair, hope;
Where there is darkness, light;
Where there is sadness, joy.

Francis of Assisi (1182–1226)

In this sad world of war
can peace be ever found?
Unless the love of Christ prevail
true peace will not abound.

The Master's new command
was: love each other well.
O people, let us all unite
to do his holy will.

Tai Jun Park

Dear Lord,
Help us to keep the world in peace and harmony
as you created it in the beginning.
Help us, Lord, to live in peace with each other,
whatever our race and colour, religion and political ideas.

God our Father,
help me not to see people
as different races,
as red
or yellow,
black
or white.
Instead
let me see them as persons
who feel,
who laugh,
who cry,
who hurt or hate or love
just as I do.

Dear Lord,
Help all the people who find it hard to love one another.
Amen

Fiona McElligott (age 8)

Where there is hatred
or hunger,
where there is guilt and despair,
where there is war and misery;
where there is hunger
and illness;
where people laugh,
and where they cry,
where they are glad,
or sad,
help us to find you, Lord,
and serve you.

Please guide the leaders of many different countries
at the meetings where they try, by working together,
to make the world a better and safer place.
Help them to want peace rather than power,
and show them how they can share the food
in the world so that no one need be hungry.

Beryl Page

Dear God our Father,
Please help people not to fight just because of colour.
Please explain to them it does not matter what colour you are,
because we are all your children, and you are our Father.
Amen

Kelly Brotherhood (age 11)

Lord, our heavenly Father,
Help us to be more loving to each other.
Jesus told us that in loving
our neighbour we are loving you.
Help us to stop wars and to start
loving one another
as you love us.
Amen

Joanna Morris (age 11)

Lord,
Bless me now
as I go out into your world.
Let me feel your love,
experience your forgiveness,
and sense your power
within me.
Give me your understanding
so that I can understand others.
Shower upon me
your hope,
your peace,
your joy.

Dear Lord,
  Help me to CARE,
    Help me to SHARE.

C.C.

Father,
I pray that people
who are rich don't keep
all the money for themselves,
but that you help them
to spend it wisely
on the starving
and poor people.
Amen

Anna Lucas (age 11)

Blessèd Lord Jesus, thou camest in poverty,
sharing a stable with beasts at thy birth;
stir us to work for thy justice and charity,
truly to care for the poor upon earth.

Patrick Appleford

Dear God,
Please help people
to understand
what is going on
in the world,
and not to be blind to
poverty and disease.
Let us help those not
as fortunate as ourselves
and treat everyone equally.
Amen

Claudia Arnold (age 11)

Lord,
You are the God of love.
Help me today to love not only my family and friends,
but all the people I meet—my teachers, my neighbours,
the people in the shops or the people on the bus.
You love them.
Help me to love them, too.
Amen

C.C.

I look at the people with labels—
those who are too fat,
too tall,
too awkward,
or too homely.
I don't really want to be friends with them, Lord.
I'd like to avoid them
if I could,
the way others do.
Yet I know you don't want me
acting that way,
for you treated the rich and the poor,
the popular and the unpopular, just the same.
Help me
so that I no longer
label others.
Help me love everyone
the way you love
all of us.

Dear God,
Help us to care more about
the community in which we live.
Make us more forgiving of others
and tolerant of their ideas and needs.
Teach us to look for the good
and to be less eager to criticize.
Help us to understand that,
even when life seems hard and unfair,
we can grow stronger through our difficulties,
and use what we learn to help our neighbours
and friends.
Amen

Father God,
We love the countryside.
We like to run in the wide, open fields
and climb the rolling hills of soothing green.
We love the tall forests and leafy woodlands,
the winding rivers and tiny streams.
Lord, we love the peace that nature brings.
Help us to value and preserve the beauty,
so that the children of the future
can enjoy it as we do today.

Heavenly Father,
Please help us to protect the wildlife
which you created for the earth.

Help us to respect animals with
love and affection, so that those
animals and insects which are becoming extinct
can live and produce more of their own breeds.

Help us also to realize that we would not like
our homes to be destroyed if we were animals.

Alexandra Allan (age 11)

Dear God,
Help us to appreciate your creation and hard work.
Some of us need to be taught how to love and respect
our birds, sea creatures and land mammals.
Please help us to care for animals around us
as if they were our relatives.
Lord hear us.
Amen

Caroline Harris (age 10)

Lord,
You are the God who cares.
You send the rain to water the land.
You give the sun to brighten our dark days.
You care for the frightened rabbit, the prowling lion,
the smallest chick and the soaring eagle.
Sometimes, Lord, we are careless.
We hunt, we trap, we tease, we destroy,
we burn, we pollute.
Please Lord, give us some of your care.
Make us carers, too.

Jodie Mason (age 10)

Dear God, please help us to keep our towns and cities clean. Teach us not to drop litter or to pollute the air by driving our cars unnecessarily.
Amen

Sophie Spring (age 10)

Dear God,
The traffic is really bad now.
We sat in the car
for an hour without moving.
The exhaust fumes were clogging
up the air so we could hardly breathe.

Lord, help us to be more sensible
about how we travel.
Give wisdom to those who are
in positions of power,
so they can do something to help.
Stop us polluting the atmosphere even more,
just because we are too lazy to think
of an alternative.

When I go to school in the morning,
I walk through rubbish each day.
Dear God, you didn't make things to
be wasted and thrown away.

You made the world to be clean,
not to be used as a dump.
You want us to use it carefully,
but people don't care at all.

Please help us to care more.
Amen

Victoria Allan (age 11)

Dirty footmarks spoil the seat on the train.
An empty beer can rolls sadly around as
the train rattles along.
Graffiti splatters the vast grey buildings outside.
Bulging dustbins spill their contents
on to the grimy streets.
Children and dogs play amongst the filth and litter.

Why don't people care any more?

Please Lord, help us to clean up our cities.
Give people respect for where they live.
Let's clean up the world.

For people who lose their homes
in storms or floods,
for those people hurt in the war
who have to live with their wounds,
for those with illnesses
the doctors can't help,
for those whose minds are sick
and can't live normally,
and for sick children
who may never get better,
dear Jesus, I pray.
Take special care of them,
just as you did when you were on earth.

PLEASE GOD, HELP...

God is our refuge and strength,
an ever-present help in trouble.

Psalm 46:1

Dear Lord,
please can you help all the
starving people in Africa.
Please give them rain,
more food to eat and strength.
Amen

Vaughan Marles (age 11)

People starving,
People not fed,
People in countries without any bread.
People dying, both young and old.
People praying for God to save them all.
Dear Lord, help them.

Louise Goodman (age 13)

Father, I want to pray for the children in the world
who don't get enough to eat.
I know there are some countries
where it hardly rains at all so nothing grows.
Or else it rains too much all of a sudden
and washes everything away.
I know you love those poor starving children
even more than I do, but you expect me to help them.
I will try to do without sweets today
and send the money I've saved to help the hungry.

Dear God,
When we are hungry,
we feel bad-tempered and cross.
We find something to eat as soon as we can.
We forget that there are parts of the world
where people are always hungry.
They cannot ever find enough to eat.
Lord, help us to remember next time we open the fridge,
that for some the hunger pains never go away.
Help us to give more to countries where there is famine.

Dear Lord,
We pray for those in Ireland
being terrorized
and those held hostage in the Middle East.
We ask for people everywhere
to have freedom to pray as we pray,
and to speak as freely as ourselves.
Help those cut off by civil war,
who are dying of starvation.
We are not only destroying our planet,
we are destroying ourselves.
Please show us the right road to peace.
Amen

Mark Carter and Grant Chamberlain (age 13)

Jesus, I pray for South Africa,
that the black people will have
as much freedom as the white.
Amen

Tim Worthley (age 11)

Lord,
You made the world perfect.
We have ruined it by being selfish.
We are sorry, Lord.
There are problems in the world which we have caused,
especially in Ireland.
I pray, Father, that you would intervene in that situation.
I pray that you will help the people of Ireland who want peace.
Thank you, Lord.
Amen

Claire O'Leary (age 12)

Lord of Heaven and Earth,
We pray for peace in the Lebanon.
Guide the leaders of that country,
the Middle East and the super-powers
to find a lasting way to stop the war there.

Please give comfort and hope to those who suffer—
whether injured, homeless, or mourning lost loved ones;
and give strength to all those who are helping them.

Build your church in the Lebanon with the lives of people
who will show your love and light,
and bring reconciliation and healing to all.
In Jesus' name,
Amen

Nabil Shehadi

Lord God,
We ask you to pour
your love
and compassion
on those held hostage
in different parts
of the world,
especially those in ....

Strengthen them in their ordeal,
give them patience and endurance,
and offer them fresh hope
for a future that will bring an end
to violence, imprisonment and suffering.

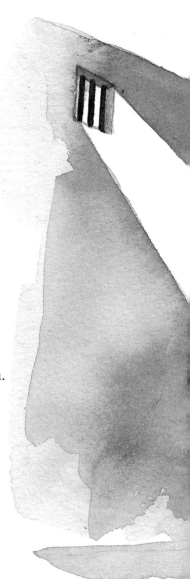

Father,
I'm worried about the hostages.
They must think that the world has forgotten them.
Some of them have to sit in the dark all day long,
and never see light.
They must get very frightened,
locked away in a strange place,
far from their homes and families.

Lord, I pray that they will feel your presence
upholding them in their fear,
and your love lighting up their darkness.
In Jesus' name,
Amen

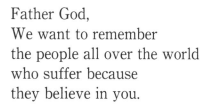

Father God,
We want to remember
the people all over the world
who suffer because
they believe in you.

We pray for those in prison,
those who are threatened or tortured,
and for those who have to worship you
secretly and in fear.

We ask you to love, bless
and strengthen them.
Give them courage.
Help them to remember
that you suffered for us
and that you feel their suffering.

Lord, be close to these people now,
wherever they may be.
Comfort them with your spirit
and give them your peace.

Lord God,
we thank you that you are father to all of us.
We ask you now to help all children
who have lost their homes
through war, flood or famine.

Help those who, because of poverty,
have been forced to leave their families
to live on the streets, fighting for
survival in the harsh and cruel cities of the world.

Love and comfort them now as they struggle.
Bless those who work to provide them
with food and shelter.
Give wisdom and compassion to those in authority,
who have the power to give aid.
In Jesus' name,
Amen

O Lord, help us who roam about. Help us who have been
placed in Africa and have no dwelling place of our own.
Give us back our dwelling place. O God, all power
is yours in heaven and earth.

Prayer of an African chief

Dear God,
Help us to set up communities
for the poor and homeless.
Help us to raise money for them,
so they can buy food and clothes.

Penelope Jones (age 11)

Dear Jesus,
You were taken as a
baby refugee into Egypt—
take care of all
the homeless wanderers,
of all who have to leave
their comfortable homes
because of the misfortunes of war,
and of all who have
no homes at all.

Guide them with your love to find
help and friends, and to help each other
in their loneliness.

Father,
We want to remember all those who are sick
at this time, either at home or in hospitals
all over the world.

We pray for those wounded in war,
  those suffering terrible diseases,
  those with handicaps which prevent
  them leading a normal life.

Lord, we pray for their pain,
  their helplessness,
  their frustration,
  their desperation.

We ask you to comfort them and soothe their pain.
May they know your healing spirit.
Let them feel your love holding them through the bad times.

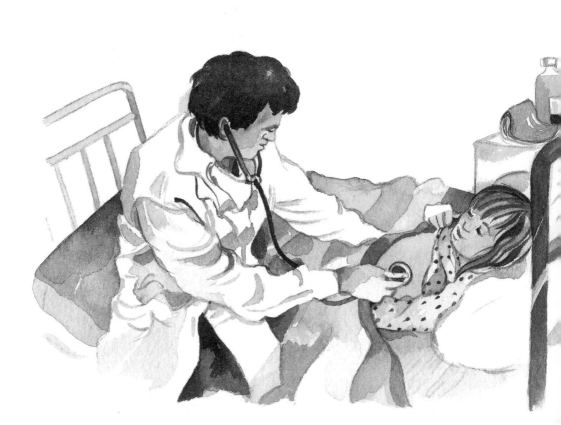

Dear Lord, I pray for people who want to commit suicide
because they are so unhappy.
Help these people to know that you love them very much
and do not want them to die.
Let them know you are there to help them with their problems.
Amen

Olga Dixon-Brown (age 12)

Lord God, we pray for the children
all over the world who are ill.
They must feel very sad sometimes
when they see their friends running about
and playing without them.
Father, we ask you to strengthen the sick.
Give them patience and courage
to overcome their problems.
Bless the nurses and doctors who help them.

Father,
We pray for all the drug addicts
who daily crave their next fix.

We pray for the alcoholics who
hourly crave the next drink.

We pray for all those who, because
they feel lonely, unloved or a failure,
search for comfort in ways that harm them.

Father, let them come to know you
and the comfort and support that
your love brings.

Please God,
Help the people who live with heavy pollution.
Clouds of toxic gases
obliterate the sun.
The forests die,
the flowers grow stunted.
Babies are born deformed and handicapped.
Children develop terrible diseases.

And yet, the factories grind on...
churning out more poison to kill and maim.

Stop them, Lord.
Help those in power to see sense.
Bless those who already
fight this evil.

Dear God, please help the people who ship oil across the sea,
which is home to the beautiful blue whale,
the exquisite coral, the waving sea anemones,
the turtles, the seals and all the fish you created.
May the captains of the ships be much more careful
when travelling across the vast ocean,
because if their ships spill any more oil
it could have a disastrous effect.
Amen

Sian Glaessner (age 11)

Father, we pray to you about the terrible pollution
of the atmosphere.
Chemicals pour from factory chimneys,
filling the air with poison.
Acid rain falls and seeps into the ground,
damaging trees, plants and the crops we eat.
It collects in streams, rivers and reservoirs,
poisoning the water we drink.
Please, Lord, we pray that you will touch the minds
of those in power all over the world.
Make them stop the pollution NOW.

Dear Father,
I look at the vast ocean
with the sunlight glinting on
its powerful waves.

I think of all the amazing
creatures which live and swim
in the depths of the sea.

Then I remember what we have
done to your creation.
We have dumped waste, spilled oil
and poisoned the water with chemicals.
We kill off life with our selfish desires.

Now we see the consequences
of our mindless destruction.

Help us, Lord, to right the wrong.
Stop people polluting the seas any more.
Make them see sense.

Lord,
Please help the elephants.
People hunt and kill them for their ivory tusks.
Soon there will be none left.
Stop the poachers, Lord, before it's too late.
Give wisdom to the people in power
who can protect the creatures you love.

It roams the thundering upper deep,
agile as a bird in the vast, empty sky.
No enemies has it, save one,
and that is man.

God of the waves,
God of the land,
God of the air,
help us to stop the whaling.

Help us to make everyone see
that all animals are here
not only to serve us,
but also for us to serve them.
Amen

Richard Edgar and Andrew Pettifer (age 13)

Heavenly Father, what we are doing to animals is dreadful...
slaughtering them for feathers, fur coats and handbags.
Help people to understand that these helpless animals
are suffering terrible deaths just to give us pleasure.
Help those who kill these animals
to realize that they are doing wrong,
and to put it right.
Amen

Katie Lane (age 10)

Dear Lord, please help people to understand animals.
Please help us to stop the cruelty to them—
and using them for experiments which may be unkind.

Teach us to be considerate and respect animals.
Everything has a right to live, not just humans.
Amen

Livia Collins (age 10)

Lord, in our greed for land and timber,
we have destroyed many forests you created.
Rare plants and animals die
and the land becomes desert.

Some people think that if we plant more trees
everything will be all right.
They don't realize that if we chop down the rainforests
they will be gone for ever.
We can never replace them.

Please God, help the people in power
to see that we cannot go on destroying your creation.
Make them understand that the world needs these trees for life.

Dear heavenly Father,
I pray that people would stop
chopping down the rainforests,
because by the time I'm an adult
the land will be a desert where
nothing will live or grow.
Amen

Daniel Marchant (age 10)

Dear God our Father,
Please don't let people destroy the rainforest,
where all the weird and wonderful animals live,
because when you made this world
you didn't want it ruined.
Amen

Louise Burke (age 10)

LORD, IN THE FUTURE...

"I will give them an undivided heart
and put a new spirit in them..."

Ezekiel 11:19

Change our hearts, Lord.
Soften them and renew them.

Rid us of our pride, and
make us more humble and open
to the views of others.

Teach us to give out and share.

Help us to know the joy that comes
from loving and caring for others
more than ourselves.
Amen

Father, I pray that somehow people will see
that we've got everything back to front.

We should learn to
talk not fight,
help not hurt,
give not take,
love not hate.

Then we will have hope for a better future together.

Dear God,
We can do nothing to change
our selfish and sinful nature.
It's just the way we are.
We need YOU to change us.
Help us to look after your world
and each other in YOUR way.
Amen

James Lynch (age 9)

O God of earth and altar
bow down and hear our cry,
our earthly rulers falter,
our people drift and die;
the walls of gold entomb us,
the swords of scorn divide,
take not thy thunder from us,
but take away our pride.

G. K. Chesterton (1874-1936)

Lord,
Help us to remember that the important things
in life are love, friendship and honesty;
and that all the money and material
things in the world will not make us happy
if we are not right in ourselves.

Give us each day a sense of how
you would like us to be, so that we may
use our lives in a way that pleases you.
Amen

No servant can serve two masters.
Either he will hate the one
and love the other,
or he will be devoted to one
and despise the other.
You cannot serve both God and money.

Luke 16:13

We are the children of the future.
We fight no wars.
We pollute no seas.
Let us lead the way.

We kill no people.
We cut down no forests.
Let us lead the way, Lord.

Trevor Smith (age 13)

Lord God,
you knew what it was like to be different...
Sometimes it's difficult
not to go along with the crowd,
even when we know they're wrong.
We have to be strong and brave.

But someone has to be first
to change from wrong to right.

Help each one of us, Lord,
to be courageous in our daily lives;
to hang on to what is good, honest and true,
and be a fine example that shines out,
so that others will want to follow our lead.

Father,
We live in a world full of fear,
hatred and selfish greed.
Help us to change our attitudes,
so that we are more interested in
the welfare of others.

Teach us to give rather than receive,
to be thankful, not critical or complaining.
Help us to praise and encourage each other
as we tackle the problems of each day.
In Jesus' name,
Amen

God,
some days I feel like a small dot
in this huge universe.
I wonder why I am here.
Is there a reason for my birth?
I can't seem to see what it is,
yet
you have given me talents,
gifts I can use
to work
for you.
Guide me
so that I see
how this tiny speck called me
can be a useful part of this world.
Show me your will
for my life.

Father,
Thank you that you gave each one of us
different abilities, roles and opportunities in this life.

Help us to be thankful for the gifts you have given us,
and to use them creatively, not for our own ends,
but humbly and gladly for your service in this world.
In Jesus' name,
Amen

As thy new horizons beckon,
Father, give us strength to be
children of creative purpose,
thinking thy thoughts after thee,
till our dreams are rich with meaning,
each endeavour, thy design:
great Creator, lead us onward
till our work is one with thine.

Catherine Bonnell Arnott

You are in charge of everything, Lord.
You made the heaven and the earth.
You know everything that happens.

Although we are often puzzled
and confused by life, we know
that you are working your purpose out
through what happens in your world.

You created us and you love us.
Help us to use the talents you
gave us to play our small part
in furthering your purpose.

Do not worry about your life,
what you will eat;
or about your body,
what you will wear.
Life is more than food,
and the body more than clothes.
Consider the ravens: they do not sow or reap,
they have no storeroom or barn;
yet God feeds them.
And how much more valuable you are than birds!

Luke 12:22-24

Lord,
Sometimes I can't sleep at night
because I'm so worried.

I worry about
 what I have said,
 what I should have said,
 what I have done,
 what I haven't done,
 what has happened,
 what could happen...

Father, I ask you to help me be less anxious.
I know that if I talked to you more about my troubles—
and let you handle them, I would be more at peace.

Help all of us to realize that you are there
to help and guide us through life,
if only we stop to listen.

Thank you, Lord.

Father God,
You made us.
You gave us the feelings of love, compassion, joy and hope.
But sometimes we feel things like
anger, hatred, sadness and despair.
Lord, these emotions sometimes make us
behave badly towards each other, and cause the problems
we have in the world today.
Help us to cope with our feelings.
Teach us to think more before we say or do
something that hurts.
Make us more honest and sensitive to others' feelings,
as well as our own.
Help us to keep love and harmony in our lives,
so that gradually this peace
will spread outwards into all the world.
In Jesus' name,
Amen

Drop thy still dews of quietness,
till all our strivings cease;
take from our souls the strain and stress,
and let our ordered lives confess
the beauty of thy peace.

John Greenleaf Whittier (1807-92)

Lord,
make me see your glory
in every place.

Michelangelo (1475-1564)

Lord, help the car-makers to produce cars
that use unleaded fuel, and factory workers
to think up a way of stopping the smoke
which the factories give off.
Amen

Kathryne Starmer (age 11)

Father God, the more that we explore the wonderful world
that you have created, the more riches we find.
The world has so much to offer, yet we are wasteful
and greedy about its resources.
Teach us to use them wisely and well.

We give you thanks for the brilliant minds of scientists and
engineers. We find it exciting to see what they are able to do,
yet we also see how easy it is to turn their discoveries
and activities to the wrong purpose. Teach us to use our skills
to create rather than to destroy, to help rather than to hinder
the progress of humanity.

All that we have is your gift. We are the stewards
of the richness of the world. Help us to make the best
possible use of it all for your glory and for the good of all people.

Dear Lord,
We pray that all the money and wealth in the world
will be more fairly distributed, and that the rich countries
will not exploit the poor, but share more with them.

We pray that those in power will think seriously
about the best use of wealth, and not waste money
on projects which are not to the good of humanity.

We pray, Father, that we will all learn to use our money
more wisely, so that it is put to the best possible use,
to help to keep your world in balance.

Father God,
You have provided everything we need.
Help scientists to discover new ways
to make power from the sun, water
and the wind.
Thank you.
Amen

Father God,
I pray that the farmers
will not use unnecessary chemicals
on their crops, and that they
will farm with care in harmony
with nature.

Lord, we pray that people will realize
the importance of recycling rubbish.

We waste paper
    dump bottles,
    scrap cars
and do not stop to think what this means.

Paper,
glass
and metal
mean trees, and precious minerals.

Father, we hope that in the future
everyone will think carefully about
re-using whatever they can to avoid
using up the world's resources.

Dear Lord,
We pray that the governments and rulers of the world
will use the power they have wisely.
Open their eyes.
Help them to see that they have a responsibility—
to you and not just to people.
We pray that the preservation of nature and conservation
should at all times be a priority in the making of decisions,
and that the nations of the world will be taught more
about how to look after the environment.
In Jesus' name,
Amen

We thank you
that if we have you
at the centre of our lives,
and try to live according
to your will,
we know that our mistakes
and failures will be forgiven.

We pray that you will help us to live
our lives creatively and positively,
in a way that is pleasing to you.

Guide us to right and wise decisions
that will bring a better future for us all.
In Jesus' name,
Amen

Give us help, Lord,
and we will pull through.
Give us hope, Lord,
and we will pull through.
Give us love, Lord,
and we will pull through.

Russell Dyke (age 13)

Dear Lord,
Thank you for giving us a promise
that you will always look after us.
I'm glad you really care for us.
I think I would like to live until I'm 100, at least!
Amen

Sharon Cuthbert (age 9)

God is love, and, though with blindness
sin afflicts our human hearts,
God's eternal loving kindness
holding, guiding, grace imparts.
Sin and death and hell shall never
o'er us final triumph gain;
God is love, so love for ever
o'er the universe must reign.

Timothy Rees (1874-1939)

Lord, we know that you are all goodness,
and that you want the best for your children.
We look forward in hope to what you
will do in the world.

Then I saw a new heaven and a new earth,
for the first heaven and the first earth
had passed away...
And I heard a loud voice from the throne saying,
'Now the dwelling of God is with men,
and he will live with them.
They will be his people, and God
himself will be with them and be their God.
He will wipe away every tear from their eyes.
There will be no more death or mourning or
crying or pain, for the old order of things has
passed away.'

Revelation 21:1, 3-4

This list supplements, and is designed to be used in conjunction with, the main contents list. Figures refer to the page on which a prayer or prayers appear. Page references for main themes are listed in bold type and are followed by references to individual prayers.

We would like to thank all those who have given us permission to include prayers in this book, as indicated on the list below. Every effort has been made to trace and contact copyright owners. If there are any inadvertent omissions in the acknowledgments we apologize to those concerned. All prayers except those acknowledged in the main text or listed below, have been written by Carol Watson. The figures refer to the page on which a prayer appears.

Augsburg Publishing House: pp.12(a), 36(a), 58, from *Lord, I Want to Tell You Something—Prayers for Boys*, Chris Jones; 17(a), 46, 49(b), 52(b), 80(a), from *Just a Minute, Lord—Prayers for Girls*, Lois Walfrid Johnson. CCA: p.45(b), from *CCA Hymnal* no. 183. Church Pastoral Aid Society: p.48(a), from *Please God*. Hodder and Stoughton Ltd: p.17(c), from *Prayers for Young Children*, Brenda Holloway. National Christian Education Council: p.85(a), from *Prayers to Use With 11–13s*. Oxford University Press: p.67(b), from *Time and Again Prayers*, compiled by Janet Cookson and Margaret Rogers. John Paul, The Preacher's Press: p.47(b), from *Short Prayers for a Long Day*, Giles and Melville Harcourt. St Paul's Publications: pp.15(a), 60(c), from *Prayers for Young People*. Veritas Publishing: p.25(c), from *Veritas Religious Education Programme—Workers for the Kingdom, Primary 7*. Joseph Weinberger: p.50(d), from *30 Twentieth-Century Hymn Tunes*, Patrick Appleford.

The author would like to thank the children and teachers of the following schools for their help and support in the making of this book:

Ferndown Middle School, Ferndown, Dorset

St Christina's Montessori School, St John's Wood, London, NW8

Notting Hill and Ealing High School, London, W13

St Joseph's RC First and Middle School, Harrow, Middlesex

St Anthony's Convent Preparatory School, Westbury, Dorset

St Luke's Primary School, West Kilburn, London, W9

Cuckfield Primary School, Cuckfield, West Sussex

The River School, Worcester

Macaulay School, Clapham, London, SW4

St Joseph's First and Middle School, London, W7

The children of the Sunday School of Holy Trinity Church, Brompton, London, SW7